ŠEVČÍK

VIOLIN STUDIES

OPUS 8

CHANGES OF POSITION AND PREPARATORY SCALE STUDIES

LAGENWECHSEL UND TONLIETER-VORSTUDIEN

CHANGEMENTS DE POSITION ET ÉTUDES PRÉPARATOIRES AUX GAMMES

BOSWORTH

BOE005163
ISBN: 978-1-84449-500-9
Music setting by Musonix

Editor: Millan Sachania

Cover design: Miranda Harvey
Cover picture: The Farmouth Stradivari, Cremona 1692 (Antonio Stradivari)
© Christie's Images Ltd.

This edition © 2004 Bosworth & Company Ltd.
Published in Great Britain by Bosworth and Company Limited

www.halleonard.com

Einer der einzigartigen Vorteile der Lagenwechsel-Übungen in Ševčíks Opus 8 ist die Einbettung jedes Lagenwechsels in einen musikalischen Zusammenhang. Das musikalische und expressive Spiel führt zu einer anderen Art der Sensibilität und zu einer höheren Reaktionsgeschwindigkeit in den Hand- und Fingermuskeln als das rein mechanische Spiel.

Während Etüden die Gelegenheit zu individuellen Lagenwechseln in einem bestimmten Musikkontext bieten, ermöglichen Übungen eine systematische Lernweise durch einfache Repetitionen und behandeln jede Möglichkeit eines Lagenwechsels auf dem Griffbrett. In seinem Opus 8 kombiniert Ševčík die Vorteile beider Herangehensweisen.

Tonhöhe, Klang, Rhythmus und Geläufigkeit.

Hören Sie aufmerksam zu, so dass Sie jeden Klang hören, der dem Instrument entspringt, und spielen Sie die Figuren in einem singenden, expressiven Ton. So wie in Tonleiterübungen, Etüden oder Stücken gibt es vier Hauptaugenmerke: Tonhöhe, Klang, Rhythmus und Geläufigkeit. Ziel ist es, jede Figur intonatorisch sauber zu spielen, mit einem reinen und expressiven Ton, mit exaktem und musikalischem Rhythmus und mit möglichst geringem Aufwand.

Während des Lagenwechsels kann das Geräusch des an der Saite entlang gleitenden Fingers von unhörbar bis expressiv reichen, abhängig von den Noten, dem Fingersatz und der musikalischen Intention.

Üben Sie auf jeder dynamischen Stufe von *p* bis *f* und achten Sie dabei darauf, dass die Finger der linken Hand locker bleiben, wenn der Bogen schwerer auf den Saiten liegt. Sie können die Expressivität jeder einzelnen Figur auch durch Crescendos und Diminuendos sowie durch Artikulationen wie *sf* steigern.

Es gibt keinen „Lagenwechsel".

In einem Buch über Lagenwechsel mag die Behauptung erstaunen, so etwas wie einen „Lagenwechsel" gebe es gar nicht; aber es gibt einen bedeutenden Unterschied zwischen dem einfachen musikalisch-expressiven Spiel von Note zu Note, siehe das Beispiel „Note–Note", und dem Einfügen eines Lagenwechsels zwischen die Noten, siehe das Beispiel „Note–Lagenwechsel–Note":

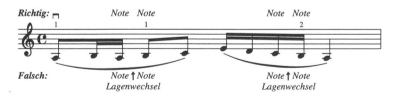

Die Note erst einmal im Geiste hören.

Hören Sie die nächste Note erst einmal innerlich, bevor Sie sie spielen, so wie es ein Sänger tut. Üben Sie das, indem Sie auf der Note vor dem Lagenwechsel eine Pause machen und im Geist die nächste Note klar hören, bevor Sie weiterspielen:

Bogenführung.

Üben Sie jede Figur sowohl mit Bindebogen als auch mit unterschiedlichen Artikulationen. Die Verwendung von Bindebögen erleichtert es, die volle Aufmerksamkeit auf die linke Hand zu legen, weg von der Bogenhand. Durch diesen Wegfall des Bogenwechsels kann das Augenmerk auf die Koordination des Lagenwechsels gerichtet werden.

Benutzen Sie in Beispiel 1 zwei Bindebögen, um zu vermeiden, dass Bogenwechsel und Lagenwechsel auf dem zweiten Schlag zusammenfallen. In Beispiel 2 mag ein Bindebogen pro Schlag natürlich und musikalisch erscheinen, vielleicht möchten Sie aber auch einen gemischten Bogenwechsel verwenden:

Oftmals ist es hilfreich, den Bogendruck während des Lagenwechsels sowie den Druck der Finger auf der Saite unmerklich zu mindern, damit man den Lagenwechsel so wenig wie möglich hört. Eine effektive Übung zur Erlangung von Geschmeidigkeit und Gleichmäßigkeit in der Bogenführung und der unabhängigen Koordination der Hände ist das gelegentliche Streichen einer Saite, während auf einer anderen gegriffen wird:

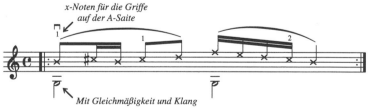

In den oberen Lagen spielen.

Da die Finger mit jedem Schritt der Übung bzw. jedem Lagenwechsel immer weiter in den oberen Saitenbereich rücken, muss der Bogen näher am Steg ansetzen, um das richtige Verhältnis von Kontaktstelle und Saitenlänge zu wahren:

Obgleich die Regel gilt, dass es mehr Bogengewicht verlangt, je näher man am Steg spielt, gilt andererseits die Regel, dass, je kürzer die Länge der Saite ist, sie umso weniger Gewicht aufnehmen kann. Daher spielen Sie insbesondere bei großen Lagenwechseln hohe Noten nahe am Steg, aber mit weniger Gewicht.

Der linke Ellbogen ist in niedrigeren Lagen weiter links positioniert und bewegt sich beim Wechsel in höhere Lagen automatisch nach rechts. Achten Sie besonders darauf, ihn wieder mehr nach links zurückzunehmen, wenn Sie wieder in niedrigere Lagen wechseln.

Koordination.

Bei gleichzeitigem Lagen- und Bogenwechsel stellen Sie sich die Note vor dem Lagenwechsel als den „alten" Finger und den „alten" Bogen, und die Note, zu der Sie wechseln, als den „neuen" Finger und den „neuen" Bogen vor. Wenn Sie auf dem alten Finger die Lage wechseln, tun Sie dies auf dem alten Bogen; wenn Sie auf dem neuen Finger die Lage wechseln, tun Sie dies auf dem neuen Bogen:

Tempo.

Jede Übung ist in Achtelnoten und Sechzehntelnoten notiert, so dass ein komplettes Lagenwechselschema immer klar abgegrenzt in einem gewöhnlichen Viervierteltakt enthalten ist, doch das sollte Ihre Wahl des Tempos nicht beeinflussen. Stellen Sie sich einmal vor, wie Sie die Übungen angehen würden, wenn Sie wie folgt notiert wären:

Die beste Herangehensweise ist es, in allen Geschwindigkeiten zu üben. Vorgeschlagene Tempi: langsam: Achtelnote = 50; mittel: Viertelnote = 50; schnell: Viertelnote = 100.

Welche Art des Lagenwechsels?

Bei einem Lagenwechsel mit dem Ausgangsfinger (auch „klassischer" Lagenwechsel genannt) verschiebt sich die Hand über dem Finger am Beginn des Lagenwechsels. Wenn die Hand in der richtigen Position ist, fällt der neue Finger direkt auf seinen Platz. Diese Lagenwechsel können aufsteigend oder absteigend gespielt werden. Die Note, auf die Sie mit dem alten Finger wechseln, bevor Sie den neuen Finger fallen lassen, wird „Zwischennote" genannt (im folgenden Musikbeispiel ist sie als Vorschlagnote abgebildet).

Bei einem Lagenwechsel mit dem Zielfinger (auch „romantischer" Lagenwechsel genannt) verschiebt sich die Hand auf dem Finger am Ende des Lagenwechsels, indem sie von unterhalb in ihn hineinrutscht. Solche Lagenwechsel werden nur aufsteigend angewandt.

Wo immer es möglich ist, versuchen Sie, jede Übung mit beiden Arten des Lagenwechsels zu üben:

Zeitliche Koordination des Lagenwechsels.

Fühlen Sie den Zielton vor dem Einsetzen des Lagenwechsels in Zusammenhang mit dem rhythmischen Gerüst. Nehmen Sie die Zeit für den Lagenwechsel von der Note davor weg. Wenn Sie die vorhergehende Note in voller Länge spielen, bleibt keine Zeit zum Lagenwechsel ohne zu spät anzukommen. Sie bewegen sich auf die neue Note ab genau dem Moment zu, in dem Sie normalerweise dort ankommen müssten. Üben Sie durch Übertreibung, indem Sie die Note vor dem Lagenwechsel kürzer als notiert spielen und die ersparte Zeit nutzen, um die Lage zu wechseln:

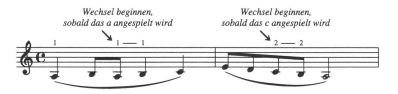

Langsame Geschwindigkeit bei der Ankunft in der neuen Note.

Wenn bei einem Lagenwechsel mit dem Zielfinger der neue Finger an der Saite hin zur neuen Note gleitet, ist es oftmals hilfreich, wenn die Geschwindigkeit des Lagenwechsels „schnell–langsam" ist. Verlagern Sie den Finger schnell zu einem Ort unweit der

Ankunftsnote und bewegen Sie ihn dann langsam weiter in die Note hinein. Üben Sie das, indem Sie die Geschwindigkeitsdifferenzen zwischen dem Anfang und dem Ende des Lagenwechsels übertreiben:

Substitutionen.

Viele Lagenwechsel sind Substitutionen, d.h. sie ersetzen einen Finger durch einen anderen auf derselben Note. Üben Sie dies, indem Sie schnell von einem Finger auf den anderen wechseln:

Verbindungen zwischen Takten.

Genauso wie Sie jeden Takt gleichmäßig und fließend spielen, verbinden Sie den Bogen am Ende eines Taktes fließend zum Beginn des nächsten. Es darf kein Akzent und keine andere Störung am Ende eines Aufstrichs entstehen:

Vibrato.

Spielen Sie ohne Vibrato und konzentrieren Sie sich auf die exakte Intonation und die Leichtigkeit der Finger auf der Saite. Spielen Sie abwechselnd auch einmal mit einem geringfügigen „Hintergrund-Vibrato", um den Klang wärmer zu machen. Üben Sie auch ein kontinuierliches Vibrato, bedacht darauf, dass es nicht am Ende einer jeden Note aufhört, sondern von einem Finger in den nächsten hineinfließt. Spielen Sie auch einmal mit einem vollen, expressiven Vibrato, so als ob die Übung einen Takt einer Sonate, eines Konzerts oder eines Streichquartetts darstellen würde.

Den Weg im Auge behalten.

Markieren Sie mit einem Haken jeden Abschnitt, den Sie bearbeitet haben. Ein Haken muss nicht bedeuten, dass der Abschnitt „perfekt" ist, nur, dass Sie ihn geübt haben. Und markieren Sie den Abschnitt mit einem weiteren Haken bei jedem weiteren Mal, dass Sie ihn wiederholt haben.

Um von der gesamten Bandbreite der Übungen zu profitieren, machen Sie jede Übung mit den elf zusätzlichen Tonarten, wie auf Seite 38 dargestellt. Schreiben Sie die Tonarten, die Sie geübt haben, an den Rand neben die Übung und notieren Sie bei jedem Spiel einen Haken.

Sollten Sie nur wenig Zeit zur Verfügung haben, können Sie wahlweise jede Übung auch nur auf einer einzigen Saite spielen: z.B. spielen Sie Nr. 1 auf der G-Saite, Nr. 2 auf der D-Saite, Nr. 3 auf der A-Saite, Nr. 4 auf der E-Saite, usw.

SIMON FISCHER
London, 2003
Übersetzung: Bosworth

One of the unique advantages of the shifting exercises in Ševčík's Opus 8 is that they provide a musical framework within which to place each shift. Playing musically and expressively triggers a different kind of sensitivity and quickness of response in the muscles in the hands and fingers from when one plays purely mechanically.

Whereas studies offer the opportunity to practise individual shifts within a musical context, exercises offer a systematic way of learning by simple repetition and of covering every instance of a shift in every area of the fingerboard. In his Opus 8, Ševčík combines the advantages of both approaches.

Pitch, Sound, Rhythm, Ease.
Listening carefully, so that you hear every sound that comes out of the instrument, play the patterns with a singing, expressive tone. Just as in playing scales, studies or pieces, there are four main headings: pitch, sound, rhythm and physical ease. The aim is to play each pattern musically in tune, with a pure and expressive tone, with exact and musical rhythm and with the least possible effort.

During the change of position, the sound of the finger gliding along the string may range from inaudible to expressive, depending on the exact notes, fingering and musical intention.

Practise at each dynamic level from *p* to *f*, taking care to keep the left fingers light when the bow sinks more heavily into the string. You can also add to the expressiveness of each pattern with crescendos and diminuendos, and articulations such as *sf*.

There is no 'shift'.
It may seem surprising to suggest that there is no such thing as a 'shift' in a book about shifting; but there is a big difference between simply playing from note to note musically and expressively, i.e. 'note–note', and inserting a shift between the notes, i.e. 'note–shift–note':

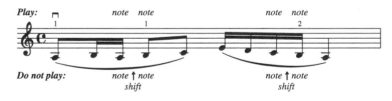

Hearing the note in your mind first.
Hear the new note in your mind before you move there, as a singer does. Practise by pausing on the note before the shift and mentally hearing the new note clearly before continuing:

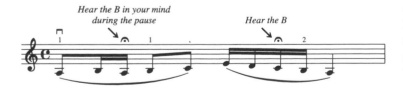

Bowing.
Practise each pattern with both slurs and separate bows. Slurring is useful for isolating the left hand from the bow, in order to avoid the

extra factors of co-ordinating the shift with the change of bow.

In No. 1, use two bows to avoid having to change bow and shift at the same time on the second beat. In No. 2, one bow to a beat may feel natural and musical, or you may wish to apply mixed bowings:

It is often good to lighten the bow infinitesimally during the shift, and to lighten the finger on the string, so that the shift is as inaudible as possible. However, as a quick practice method for improving smoothness and evenness in the bow, and independence of the hands, occasionally bow on one string while fingering another:

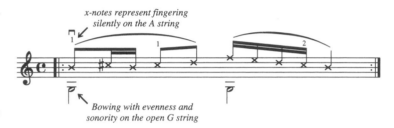

Playing high up the string.
As the fingers play higher up the string with each next step of the exercise or with each shift, the bow must play nearer to the bridge in order to keep the correct proportions of point-of-contact to length of string:

Although one principle is that playing closer to the bridge requires more bow weight than playing further from the bridge, another principle is that the shorter the string length the less weight the string can take. Therefore, especially when playing long shifts, play high notes close to the bridge but with less weight.

The left elbow is positioned more to the left in lower positions, and naturally moves to the right when shifting up into high positions. Take great care to allow it to return more to the left when shifting down again.

Co-ordination.
In separate-bow shifts, think of the note before the shift as the 'old' finger and bow, and the note to which you are shifting as the 'new' finger and bow. When you shift on the old finger, shift on the old bow; when you shift on the new finger, shift on the new bow:

Tempo.

Each exercise is notated in quavers and semiquavers, so that one complete shifting pattern is always neatly contained within one bar of common time, but this should not influence your choice of tempo. Imagine how you would approach the exercises if they were presented as follows:

The best approach is to practise at all speeds. Suggested tempi are as follows: slow: quaver = 50; medium: crotchet = 50; fast: crotchet = 100.

Which type of shift?

In a 'Beginning' shift (also called a 'Classical' shift), the hand shifts on the finger beginning the shift. When the hand is in the right position, the new finger drops directly onto its note. These shifts can be played ascending or descending. The note you shift to on the old finger, before dropping the new finger, is called an 'intermediate note' (shown as a grace note in the music example below).

In an 'End' shift (also called a 'Romantic shift'), the hand shifts on the finger that ends the shift, sliding in to it from beneath. These shifts are used only for ascending shifts.

Wherever possible, practise each exercise with both shifts:

Timing the shift.

Always feel the arrival note of the shift in relation to the underlying rhythmic pulse. Take the time for the shift from the note before the shift. If you play the previous note for its full length, there is no time to shift without arriving late; you begin to move towards the new note at the precise moment that you should actually be arriving on it. Practising by exaggeration, play the note before the shift shorter than written, and use the extra time to make the shift:

Slow arrival speed.

When the new finger glides along the string to the new note in an 'End' shift, it is often helpful if the speed of the shift is 'fast–slow'. Shift very quickly to a place somewhere below the arrival note and then continue slowly into the note. Practise by exaggerating the difference between the beginning of the shift and the end:

Substitutions.

Many of the shifts are substitutions, i.e. you replace one finger with another finger on the same note. Practise these by playing rapidly from one finger to the other:

Connexions between bars.

As well as playing each measure evenly and smoothly, at the end of one measure connect the bow smoothly to the beginning of the next. There must be no 'bump' or other disturbance at the end of the up-bow:

Vibrato.

Play without vibrato, concentrating on exactness of intonation and the lightness of the finger on the string. Play also with a minimal 'background vibrato' to warm the sound. Practise continuity of vibrato, making sure that it does not stop at the end of each note but flows from one finger into the next. Play also with a full, expressive vibrato, as though the note pattern constitutes a bar from a sonata, concerto or string quartet.

Keeping track.

Mark with a tick every section you work on. A tick does not have to mean that the section is 'perfect', only that you have practised it. Give the section another tick every time you revisit it.

To benefit from the full range of the exercises, practise each exercise in the eleven additional keys shown on page 38. Write the key signature that you have practised in the margin next to the exercise, giving it another tick each time you play it.

When time is limited, one approach is to play each exercise on only one string: e.g. play No. 1 on the G string, No. 2 on the D string, No. 3 on the A string, No. 4 on the E string, and so on.

SIMON FISCHER
London, 2003

L'un des atouts exceptionnels des exercices de déplacements de l'Opus 8 de Ševčík est d'inscrire chacun d'eux dans un cadre musical. L'exécution musicale et expressive procure une sensibilité et une rapidité de réponse des muscles de la main et des doigts d'une toute autre nature que l'exécution purement mécanique.

Les études offrent la possibilité d'effectuer chaque déplacement à l'intérieur d'un contexte musical, tandis que les exercices dispensent un apprentissage fondé sur la simple répétition et recouvrant l'intégralité des configurations d'un déplacement dans chaque position de touche. Dans son Opus 8, Ševčík réunit les avantages de ces deux formes d'approche.

Hauteur, sonorité, rythme, aisance.

En vous écoutant attentivement, de manière à percevoir tous les sons produits par votre instrument, jouez les formules avec une sonorité chantante et expressive. De même que pour l'exécution des gammes, quatre points essentiels sont à considérer: la hauteur de son, la sonorité, le rythme et l'aisance physique. Votre objectif consiste à exécuter chaque formule musicalement, à sa hauteur juste, avec un son pur et expressif, un rythme exact et musical et en fournissant le moins possible d'efforts.

Au cours des changements de position, le son du glissement du doigt le long de la corde peut être inaudible ou faire partie de l'expression selon les notes jouées, le doigté pratiqué et l'intention musicale poursuivie.

Travaillez les exercices à tous les niveaux de nuances dynamiques, de *p* à *f*, en prenant soin de maintenir la légèreté des doigts de la main gauche lorsque l'archet s'appuie plus lourdement sur la corde. Vous pouvez également augmenter l'expressivité de chaque formule par des *crescendo*, des *diminuendo* et des articulations telles que *sf*.

Le 'déplacement' n'existe pas.

Une telle affirmation peut paraître paradoxale dans un ouvrage consacré au déplacement, mais il existe une grande différence entre passer simplement d'une note à l'autre avec musicalité et expression, à savoir 'note–note', et introduire un démanché entre les notes, à savoir 'note–démanché–note':

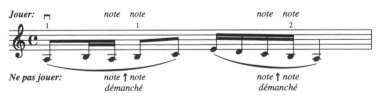

Audition intérieure d'abord.

Efforcez-vous d'entendre la note intérieurement avant de l'atteindre, selon la même démarche que celle d'un chanteur. Entraînez-vous à vous arrêter sur la note précédant le déplacement et à entendre mentalement la nouvelle note clairement avant de poursuivre:

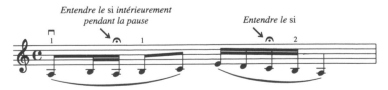

Coups d'archet.

Travaillez chaque formule mélodique sur un seul coup d'archet, puis avec des coups d'archet séparés. Le jeu lié est utile pour dissocier la main gauche de l'archet de manière à éviter la démarche supplémentaire de coordination du démanché et du changement de coup d'archet.

Dans l'exercice no. 1, pratiquez deux coups d'archet pour éviter de démancher et changer de coup d'archet simultanément sur le deuxième temps. Dans l'exercice no. 2, un coup d'archet par temps paraît une solution naturelle et musicale. Vous pouvez également, si vous le désirez, effectuer des coups d'archet croisés:

Il est souvent préconisé d'à peine alléger l'archet pendant le démanché et de relâcher la pression des doigts sur la corde de façon à rendre le déplacement aussi silencieux que possible. Cependant l'on peut occasionnellement frotter une corde tandis que l'en on doigte une autre comme exercice rapide pour améliorer la douceur et l'égalité de l'archet et l'indépendance de mains:

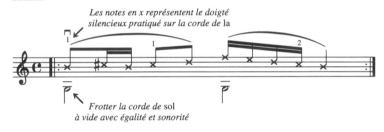

Jouer en haut de la corde.

Plus les doigts jouent vers le haut de la corde, au fur et à mesure de la progression de l'exercice, plus l'archet doit se placer près du chevalet afin de maintenir une proportion correcte entre le point de contact et la longueur de corde:

En dépit du principe qui veut que jouer près du chevalet réclame plus de pression de l'archet que jouer loin du chevalet, un autre principe impose que plus la longueur de corde est réduite moins elle peut supporter de poids. Il faut donc jouer les notes aiguës près du chevalet avec peu de pression, surtout lors des déplacements longs.

Le coude gauche se déporte vers la gauche dans les positions graves et se meut naturellement vers la droite lors des déplacements vers les positions aiguës. Prenez grand soin de reprendre la position du coude vers la gauche en redescendant dans les positions graves.

Coordination.

Lors des coups d'archet séparés, représentez-vous la note précédant le démanché comme pratiquant le doigté et le coups d'archet 'précédents' et la note vers laquelle vous vous déplacez comme pratiquant le doigté et le coup d'archet 'suivants'. Tout déplacement sur le doigté précédent implique le coup d'archet précédent et, de même, tout déplacement sur le doigté suivant implique le coup d'archet suivant:

Tempo.

Tous les exercices sont notés en croches et doubles croches de manière à inscrire chaque formule dans une mesure à 4/4. Ceci ne doit cependant pas influencer votre choix de tempo. Imaginez quelle serait votre approche des exercices s'ils se présentaient ainsi:

La meilleure méthode consiste à travailler à différents mouvements. Nous suggérons pour le mouvement lent, la croche à 50; pour le mouvement moyen, la noire à 50; pour le mouvement rapide, la noire à 100.

Quel type de déplacement?

Dans le démanché 'initial' (aussi appelé 'classique'), la main se déplace sur le doigt qui commence la démanché. Quand la main a atteint la bonne position, le nouveau doigt s'abaisse directement sur la note. Ces déplacements peuvent être réalisés dans les mouvements ascendants et descendants. La note vers laquelle on se déplace sur le doigt précédent, avant d'abaisser le doigt suivant, s'appelle 'note intermédiaire' (notée en broderie dans l'exemple musical ci-dessous).

Lors du démanché 'final' (aussi appelé 'romantique'), la main se déplace sur le doigt qui termine le déplacement en glissant d'en dessous. Ce déplacement ne s'effectue que dans les mouvements ascendants.

Travaillez ces exercices avec les deux types de déplacements, lorsque que cela est possible:

Ajustement rythmique du déplacement.

Il convient de toujours anticiper la note d'arrivée du déplacement en relation avec la pulsation rythmique sous-jacente. Commencez le déplacement sur la note qui le précède car, si vous jouez la durée complète de celle-ci, vous ne pourrez effectuer le démanché sans retard: vous aurez, en effet, amorcé votre déplacement vers la note suivante au moment précis où vous auriez dû l'atteindre. Entraînez-vous, en exagérant, à jouer la note précédant le démanché plus courte que sa durée écrite et effectuez le déplacement pendant le temps ainsi libéré:

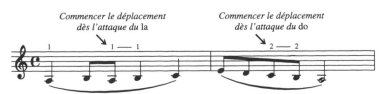

Ralentissement au terme du déplacement.

Lorsque le doigt suivant glisse le long de la corde vers la note suivante en effectuant un démanché 'final', le déplacement est souvent facilité par un mouvement 'rapide–lent'. Déplacez-vous très rapidement vers un endroit situé en dessous de la note à atteindre puis poursuivez lentement vers cette note. Travaillez en exagérant la différence entre le départ et l'arrivée du démanché:

Substitutions.

Nombre de démanchés consistent en substitutions remplaçant un doigt par un autre sur la même note. Travaillez ces substitutions en passant rapidement d'un doigt à l'autre:

Transition entre les mesures.

Jouez chaque mesure avec égalité et aisance et, à la fin d'une mesure, amenez l'archet sans heurt au début de la mesure suivante. Aucun soubresaut ni autre secousse ne doivent perturber l'aboutissement du poussé:

Vibrato.

Jouez sans vibrato, en vous concentrant sur la justesse de l'intonation et la légèreté du doigt sur la corde, tout en pratiquant un 'vibrato d'arrière-plan' minimal. Travaillez la continuité de ce vibrato en vous assurant qu'il ne s'interrompt pas à la fin de chaque note mais passe d'un doigt à l'autre. Exercez-vous également à un vibrato plein et expressif en imaginant que la formule constitue une mesure de sonate, de concerto ou de quatuor à cordes.

Garder les traces de votre travail.

Indiquez d'une marque chaque section que vous travaillez. Une marque ne signifie pas nécessairement que vous exécutez la section parfaitement mais que vous l'avez étudiée. Signalez d'une autre marque chaque fois que vous reprenez cette section.

Pour tirer le meilleur bénéfice de l'ensemble de ces exercices, travaillez chacun d'eux dans les onze tonalités indiquées page 38. Inscrivez les tonalités que vous avez travaillées en marge de l'exercice et signalez d'une marque chaque fois que vous y revenez.

Si l'on dispose de peu de temps, la méthode consiste à jouer chaque exercice sur une seule corde: no. 1 sur la corde de sol, no. 2 sur la corde de *ré*, no. 3 sur la corde de *la*, no. 4 sur la corde de *mi*, etc.

SIMON FISCHER
London, 2003
Traduction: Agnès Ausseur

Uno dei vantaggi particolari degli esercizi di cambio di posizione di Ševčík è quello di fornire una struttura musicale in cui è possibile includere ogni cambio di posizione. Se si suona con musicalità ed espressività si crea una reazione più immediata e sensibile nei muscoli delle mani e delle dita, cosa che non avviene quando si suona solo meccanicamente.

Se gli studi offrono l'opportunità di approfondire la conoscenza dei cambi di posizione individuali contenuti in un contesto musicale, gli esercizi offrono un modo sistematico di apprendimento grazie alla semplice ripetizione di ogni esempio relativo a ciascuna area della tastiera. In questa Opus 8, Ševčík unisce i vantaggi di entrambi gli approcci.

Intonazione, Suono, Ritmo, Agilità.

Ascoltare con attenzione, in modo da sentire ogni suono proveniente dallo strumento, suonare i vari schemi con un'intonazione cantabile ed espressiva. Per esempio, nel suonare le scale, gli studi o i brani tener presente i quattro titoli: intonazione, suono, ritmo e agilità fisica. L'obbiettivo è suonare ogni esercizio in modo musicale e intonato, con esattezza e ritmo musicale e con il minimo sforzo possibile.

Durante il cambio di posizione, il dito che scivola lungo la corda può emettere suoni che vanno dall' inudibile all'espressivo, a seconda delle note esatte della diteggiatura e dell'intenzione musicale.

Studiare a tutti i livelli dinamici da *p* a *f*, avendo cura di tenere le dita della mano sinistra leggere quando l'arco preme più pesantemente sulla corda. E' possibile anche aumentare l'espressività di ciascuno schema con dei crescendi e diminuendi, e articolazioni quali *sf*.

Non c'é 'cambio di posizione'.

Può sembrare strano suggerire che non ci sia alcun 'cambio di posizione' in un manuale dedicato ai 'cambi di posizione'; ma esiste una grossa differenza tra il suonare semplicemente una nota dopo l'altra con musicalità ed espressione, cioé 'nota–nota', e l'inseririmento di un cambio di posizione tra le note, cioè nota–cambio di posizione–nota:

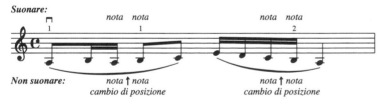

Sentire mentalmente la nota prima di suonare.

Sentire la nota nuova nella mente prima di suonarla, come fanno i cantanti. Studiare facendo una pausa sulla nota prima del cambio di posizione e sentire mentalmente la nuova nota con chiarezza prima di continuare.

Arcate.

Studiare ogni esercizio con arcate legate e separate. Le arcate legate sono utili per l'isolamento della mano sinistra dall'arco, al fine di evitare l'ulteriore problema di coordinamento del cambio di posizione con il cambio d'arco.

Nel n. 1, usare due arcate per evitare di cambiare l'arco e cambiare posizione contemporaneamente nella seconda battuta. Nel n. 2 è possibile usare in modo più naturale e musicale un'arcata per ciascuna battuta. Alternativamente si potrebbe preferire l'applicazione di arcate diverse:

Spesso è bene alleggerire un pò l'arco durante il cambio di posizione e alleggerire il dito sulla corda, in modo che il cambio sia il più inudibile possibile. Comunque, un metodo veloce e pratico per aumentare l'uniformità e lo scorrimento dell'arco e l'indipendenza di entrambe le mani, è archeggiare di tanto in tanto su una corda mentre si diteggia un'altra:

Suonare verso la parte superiore della corda.

Mentre le dita avanzano verso l'alto della corda con ogni esercizio progressivo e con ogni cambio di posizione, l'arco deve suonare più vicino al ponticello onde mantenere la corretta proporzione tra il punto-di-contatto e l'intera corda.

Sebbene uno dei principi detti che se si suona più vicino al ponticello la pressione sull'arco deve essere superiore a quella necessaria quando si suona più lontano dal ponticello, un altro principio detta che più corta è la corda meno necessaria è la pressione sulla corda. Pertanto, specialmente nel caso in cui si suonino lunghi cambi di posizione, si devono suonare le note alte più vicino al ponticello ma con meno pressione.

Il gomito sinistro è posizionato più a sinistra nelle posizioni basse, spostandosi naturalmente verso la destra nelle posizioni alte. E' necessario prestare la massima attenzione onde ritornare ad una posizione più a sinistra quando si cambia di nuovo verso il basso.

Co-ordinamento.

Nei cambi di posizione con arcate separate, bisogna pensare alla nota precedente al cambio come all'arcata del 'vecchio' dito, ed alla nota nuova come all'arcata del dito 'nuovo':

Tempo.

Ogni eserciizio è illustrato con crome e semicrome in modo da contenere lo schema completo di cambi di posizione in una sola battuta di tempo comune; questo comunque non dovrebbe influenzare la scelta del vostro tempo. Immaginate come affrontereste l'esercizio se si presentasse come segue:

Il migliore approccio è lo studio in tutti i tempi possibili. Si suggeriscono i seguenti tempi: lento: croma = 50; medio: semiminima = 50; veloce: semiminima = 100.

Quale tipo di cambio di posizione?

Nel cambio di posizione 'iniziale' (anche denominato 'classico'), la mano cambia posizione col dito che dà inizio al cambio. Quando la mano è nella giusta posizione, il nuovo dito cade direttamente sulla giusta nota. Questi cambi possono essere suonati in ascesa o discesa. La nota che cambia col vecchio dito, prima di far cadere il nuovo dito, si chiama 'nota intermedia' (dimostrata come nota d'abbellimento nell'esempio musicale sotto elencato).

In un cambio di posizione (Finale) (anche chiamato 'cambio di posizione Romantico'), la mano cambia posizione sul dito che completa il cambio, facendolo scivolare dal di sotto. Questi portamenti sono solo usati nel caso di cambi di posizione in ascesa.

Questi sono gli esempi da studiare con entrambi i cambi di posizione:

Determinare il tempo giusto del cambio di posizione.

Bisogna sentire sempre la nota d'arrivo in relazione alla pulsazione ritmica di base quando si cambia posizione. Per avere abbastanza tempo per il cambio di posizione abbreviare la nota precedente. Se si suona tale nota nella sua interezza si arriva in ritardo sulla prossima nota del cambio di posizione; incominciare a spostarsi verso la nuova nota nel preciso istante in cui si dovrebbe arrivare sulla nota. Esagerare lo studio suonando la nota accorciata prima del cambio di posizione usando il tempo extra per il cambio di posizione:

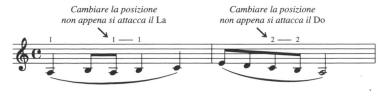

Tempo d'arrivo rallentato.

Quando il dito nuovo scivola lungo la corda per arrivare verso la nota 'finale', può essere d'aiuto se il tempo del cambio di posizione

è 'veloce–lento'. Effettuare il cambio di posizione in modo veloce posizionandosi al di sotto della nota d'arrivo e poi continuare lentamente verso la nota. Studiare esagerando la differenza tra l'inizio e la fine del cambio di posizione:

Sostituzioni.

Molti dei cambi di posizione sono sostituzioni, per esempio si sostituisce un dito con un altro sulla stessa nota. Studiare questi cambi suonando rapidamente prima con un dito e poi con l'altro:

Collegamenti tra battute.

Non si deve solo suonare ogni misura in modo uniforme ed omogeneo, ma alla fine di una misura collegare l'arco uniformemente con l'inizio della prossima. Non deve esserci alcun balzo o intoppo alla fine dell'arcata in su:

Vibrato.

Suonare senza vibrato, concentrandosi sull'esatta intonazione e la leggerezza del dito sulla corda. Suonare inoltre con un minimo vibrato di fondo per produrre un suono caldo. Studiare un vibrato continuo, facendo attenzione a che non ci sia interruzione alla fine di ogni nota ma che ci sia continuità tra un dito e l'altro. Suonare con un vibrato pieno ed espressivo, come se la serie di note costituisse una battuta di una sonata, di un concerto o quartetto.

Tenere nota del materiale studiato.

Annotare ogni battuta studiata. L'annotazione non deve significare che la sezione sia 'perfetta', ma solo che è stata studiata. Marcare la sezione nuovamente ogni volta che si studia.

Per trarre beneficio dall'intera gamma di esercizi a disposizione, studiare ogni esercizio nelle undici chiavi aggiuntive illustrate a pagina 38. Annotare la chiave studiata al margine dell'esercizio, marcandolo ogni qualvolta lo si suona.

Quando si ha un tempo limitato, un approccio è dato dallo studio di ciascun esercizio su una sola corda: cioè suonare n. 1 sulla corda del *sol*, n. 2 sulla corda del *re*, n. 3 sulla corda del *la* e n. 4 sulla corda del *mi*, e così via.

SIMON FISCHER
London, 2003
Traduzione: Anna Maggio

OPUS 8

CHANGES OF POSITION AND
PREPARATORY SCALE STUDIES

LAGENWECHSEL UND
TONLIETER-VORSTUDIEN

CHANGEMENTS DE POSITION
ET ÉTUDES PRÉPARATOIRES
AUX GAMMES

2

Lagenwechsel	**Changes of position**	**Changements de position**	**Cambiamento di posizione**
Übe Nr. 1–56 in einem mäßigen Tempo und auf folgende Art: a) jeder Takt einzeln; b) zwei aufeinander folgende Takte zusammen, z.B. die Takte 1–2, 2–3, 3–4, u.s.w.; c) alle Takte einer Zeile, z.B. die Takte 1–6, 7–12, 13–18 und 19–25 der Übung Nr. 1; d) alle Takte in den unten angegebenen Tonarten, legato und staccato.	Practise Nos. 1–56 at a moderate tempo and in the following ways: a) each bar separately; b) two consecutive bars at a time, e.g. bars 1–2, 2–3, 3–4, etc. c) all the bars lying on the same string, e.g. bars 1–6, 7–12, 13–18 and 19–25 of No. 1; d) the entire number in the keys indicated below, legato and staccato.	Travaillez les Nos. 1 à 56 dans un mouvement modéré et des façons suivantes: a) chaque mesure séparément; b) deux mesures consécutives à la fois, par ex. mesures 1–2, 2–3, 3–4, etc.; c) toutes les mesures jouées sur la même corde, par ex. mesures 1–6, 7–12, 13–18 et 19–25 du No. 1; d) l'exercice entier dans les tonalités indiquées ci-dessous, legato et staccato.	Studiare dal N. 1 al N. 56 in tempo moderato e nei seguenti modi: a) ciascuna battuta separatamente; b) due battute consecutive per volta, cioè battute 1–2, 2–3, 3–4, ecc.; c) tutte le battute si trovano sulla stessa corda, cioè battute 1–6, 7–12, 13–18 e 19–25 del N. 1; d) L'intero numero nelle chiavi sottoindicate, sia legato che staccato.

No. 1

Lagenwechsel: von der 1. zur 2., 2. zur 3., 3. zur 4., u.s.w.	Changes of position: from 1st to 2nd, 2nd to 3rd, 3rd to 4th, etc.	Changements de position: de la 1ère à la 2ème, 2ème à 3ème, 3ème à 4ème, etc.	Cambiamento di posizione: dalla 1^{a} alla 2^{a}, 2^{a} alla 3^{a}, 3^{a} alla 4^{a}, ecc.

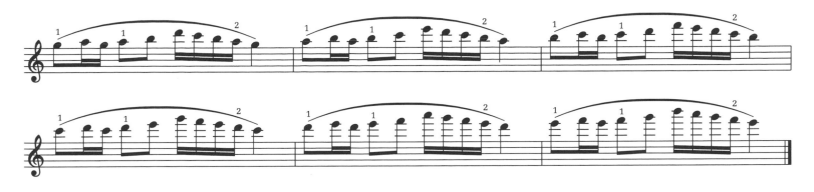

No. 2

No. 3

No. 4

No. 5

6

No. 6

No. 7

No. 8

Lagenwechsel: von der 1. zur 3., 2. zur 4., 3. zur 5., u.s.w.	Changes of position: from 1st to 3rd, 2nd to 4th, 3rd to 5th, etc.	Changements de position: de la 1ère à la 3ème, 2ème à 4ème, 3ème à 5ème, etc.	Cambiamento di posizione: dalla 1^{a} alla 3^{a}, 2^{a} alla 4^{a}, 3^{a} alla 5^{a}, ecc.

No. 9

No. 10

No. 11

No. 12

No. 13

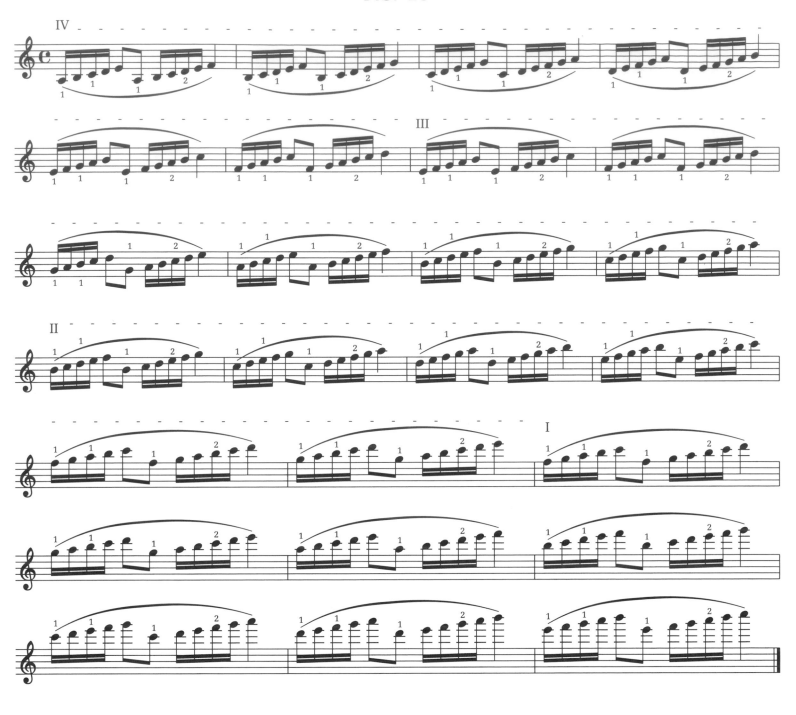

No. 14

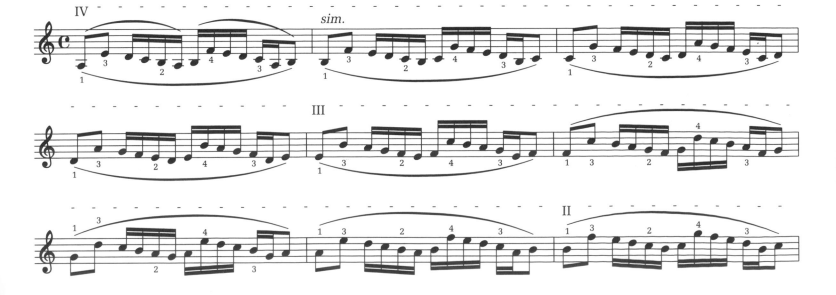

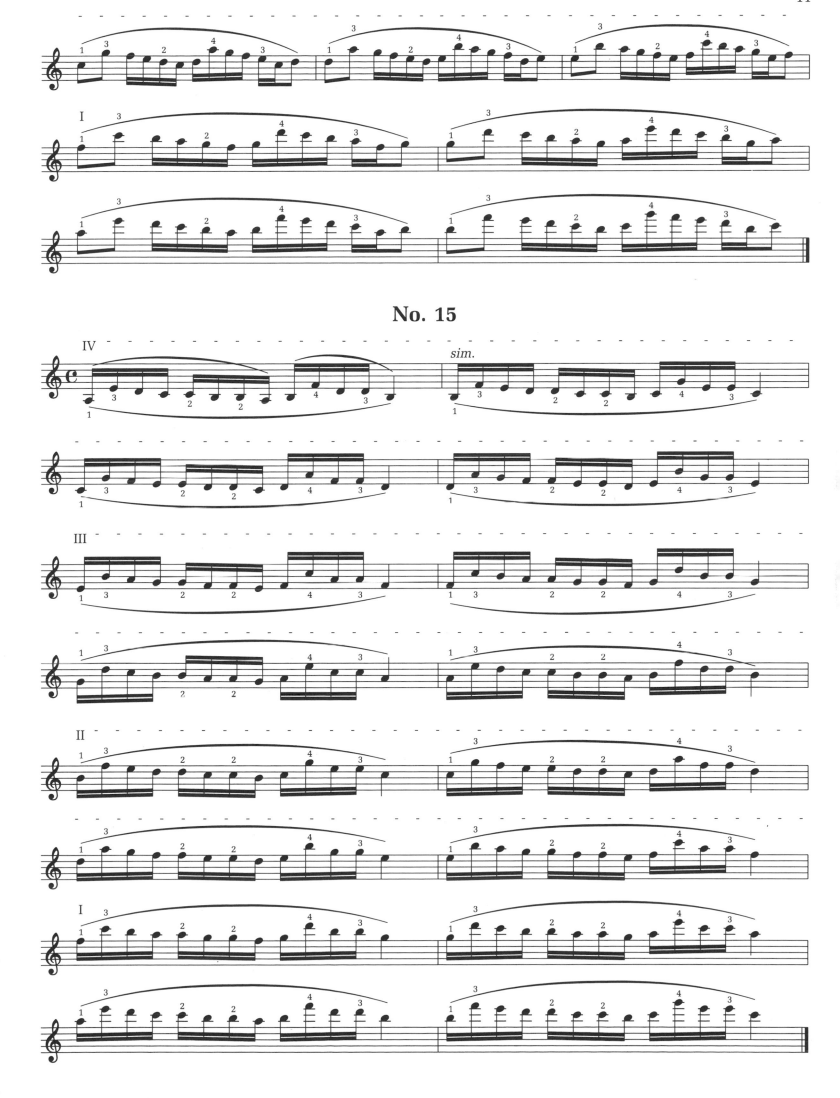

No. 15

12

No. 16

Lagenwechsel:
von der 1. zur 4., 2. zur 5.,
3. zur 6., u.s.w.

Changes of position:
from 1st to 4th, 2nd to 5th,
3rd to 6th, etc.

Changements de position:
de la 1ère à la 4ème, 2ème à 5ème,
3ème à 6ème, etc.

Cambiamento di posizione:
dalla 1a alla 4a, 2a alla 5a,
3a alla 6a, ecc.

No. 17

No. 18

No. 19

14

No. 20

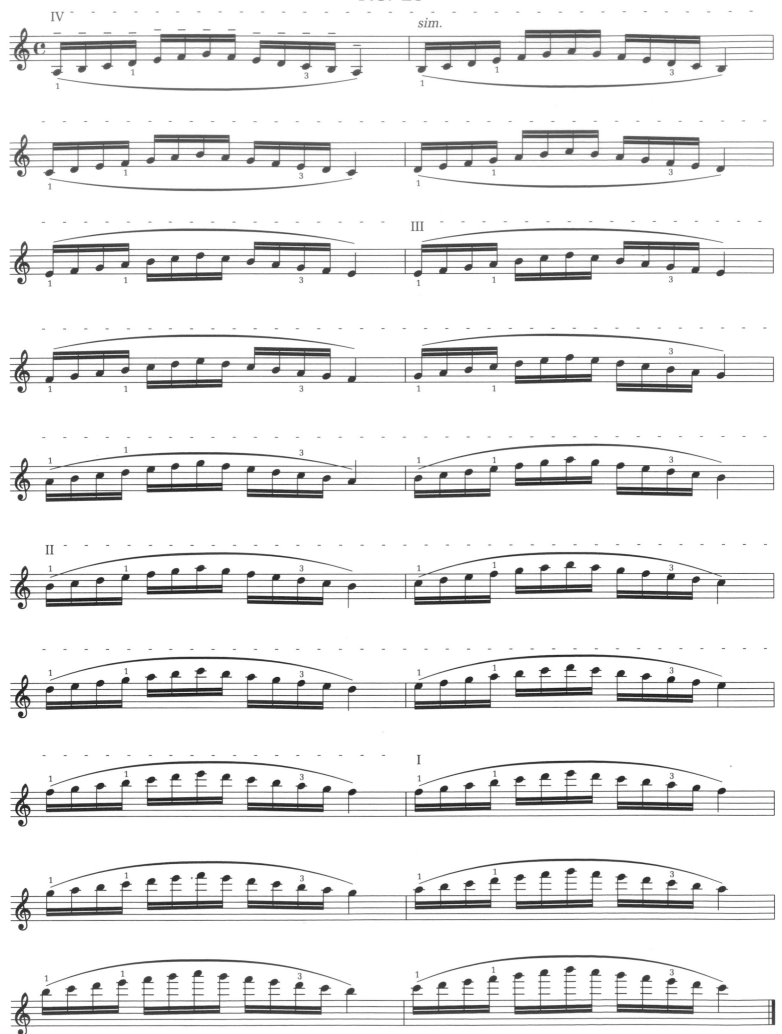

No. 21

No. 22

16

No. 23

Lagenwechsel:
von der 1. zur 5., 2. zur 6.,
3. zur 7., u.s.w.

Changes of position:
from 1st to 5th, 2nd to 6th,
3rd to 7th, etc.

Changements de position:
de la 1ère à la 5ème, 2ème à 6ème,
3ème à 7ème, etc.

Cambiamento di posizione:
dalla 1ª alla 5ª, 2ª alla 6ª,
3ª alla 7ª, ecc.

No. 24

No. 25

No. 26

No. 27

No. 28

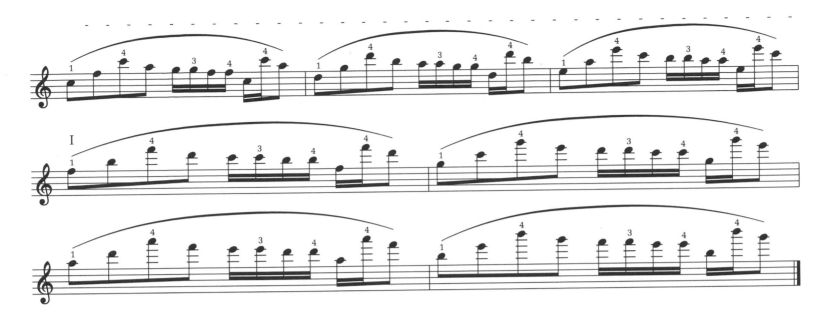

No. 29

No. 30

No. 31

No. 32

Lagenwechsel: von der 1. zur 6., 2. zur 7., 3. zur 8., u.s.w.	Changes of position: from 1st to 6th, 2nd to 7th, 3rd to 8th, etc.	Changements de position: de la 1ère à la 6ème, 2ème à 7ème, 3ème à 8ème, etc.	Cambiamento di posizione: dalla 1a alla 6a, 2a alla 7a, 3a alla 8a, ecc.

No. 33

No. 34

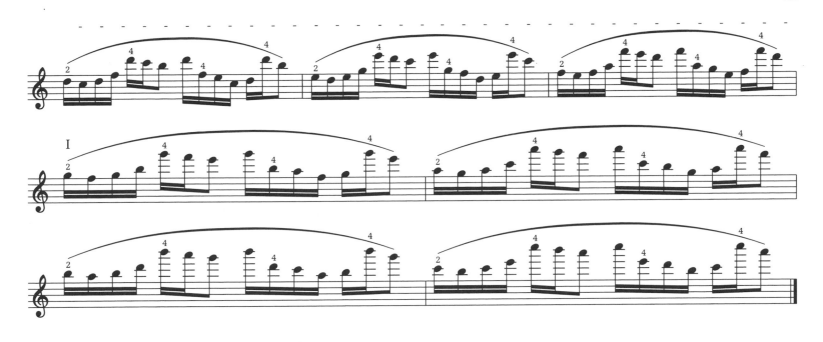

No. 35

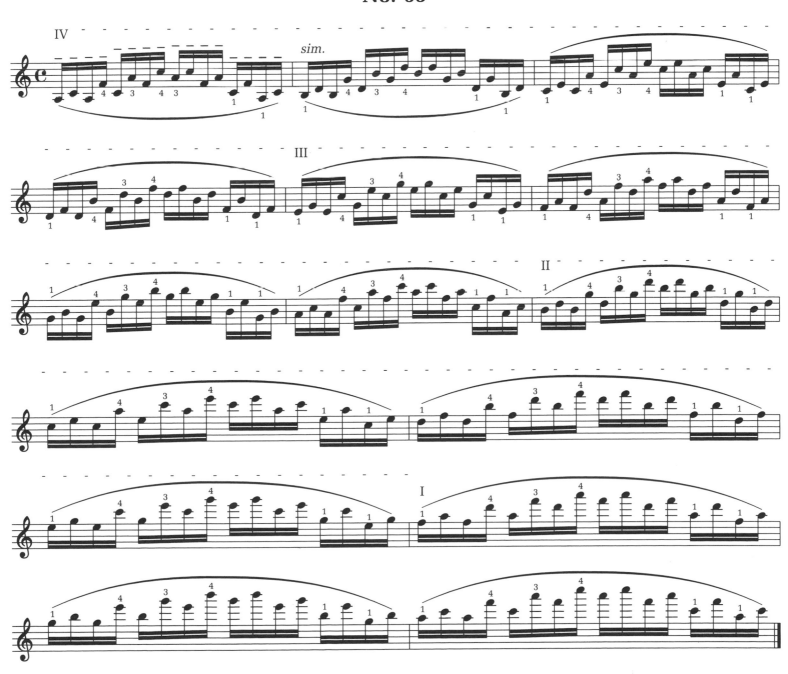

No. 36

No. 37

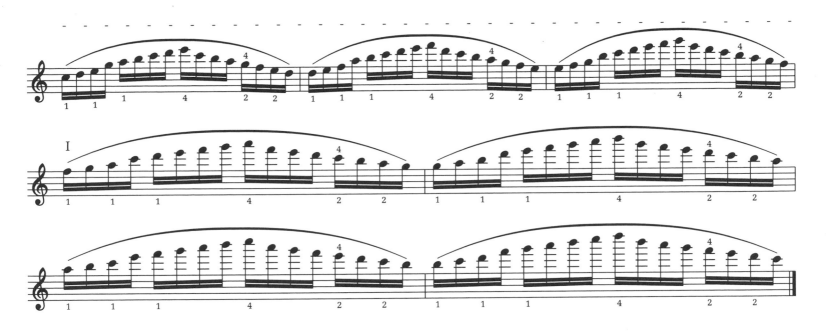

No. 38

| Lagenwechsel: von der 1. zur 7., 2. zur 8., 3. zur 9., u.s.w. | Changes of position: from 1st to 7th, 2nd to 8th, 3rd to 9th, etc. | Changements de position: de la 1ère à la 7ème, 2ème à 8ème, 3ème à 9ème, etc. | Cambiamento di posizione: dalla 1^{a} alla 7^{a}, 2^{a} alla 8^{a}, 3^{a} alla 9^{a}, ecc. |

No. 39

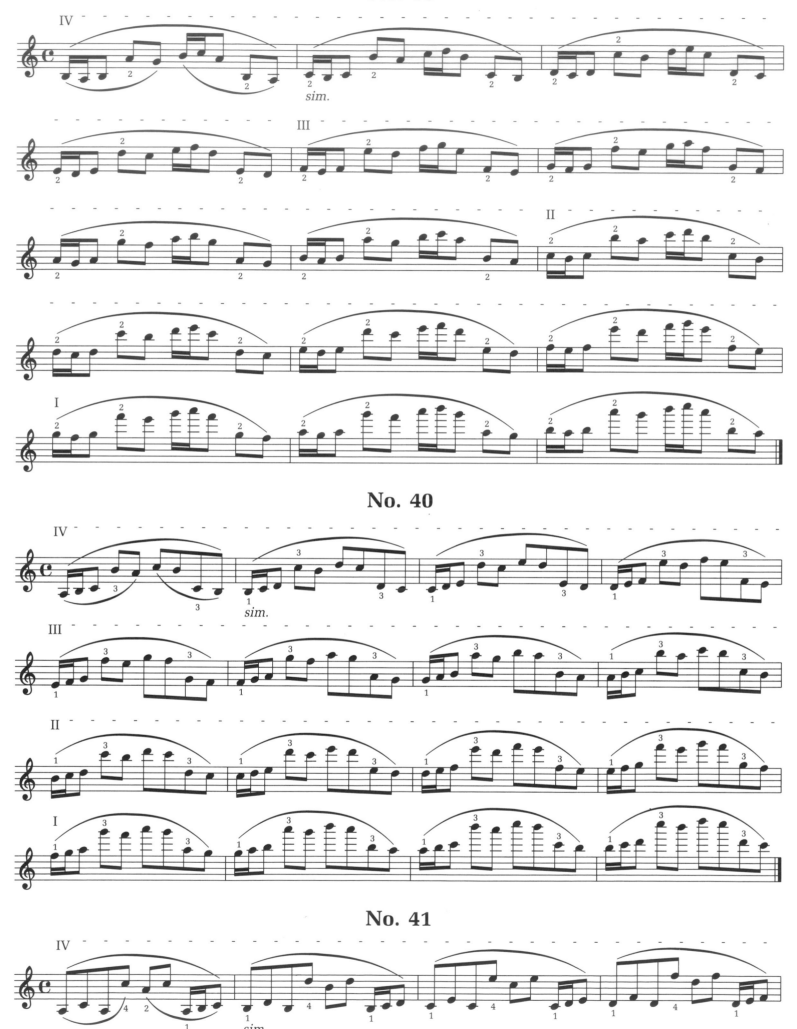

No. 40

No. 41

No. 42

No. 43

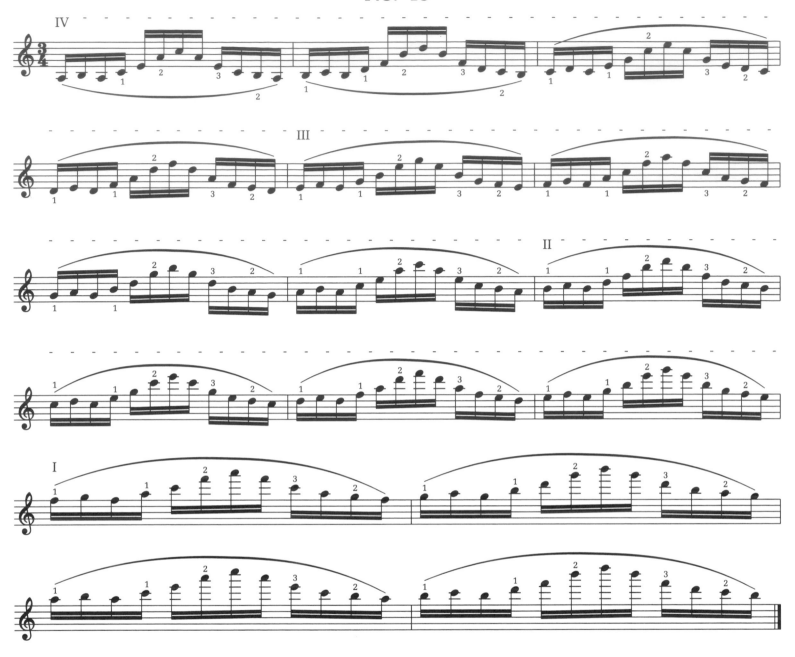

No. 44

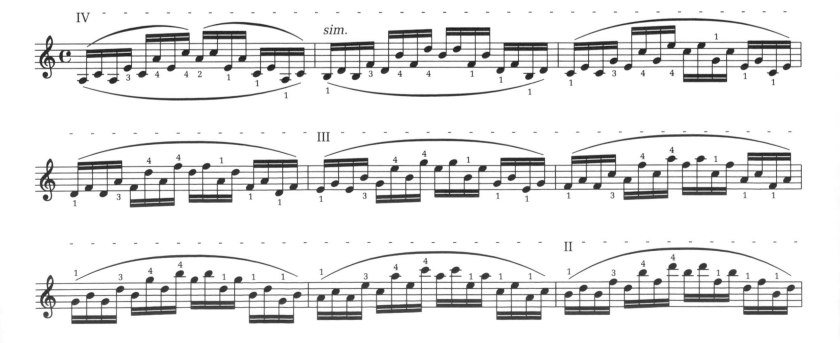

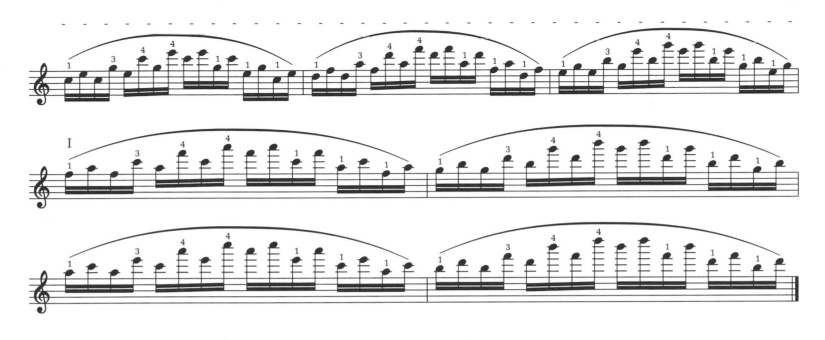

No. 45

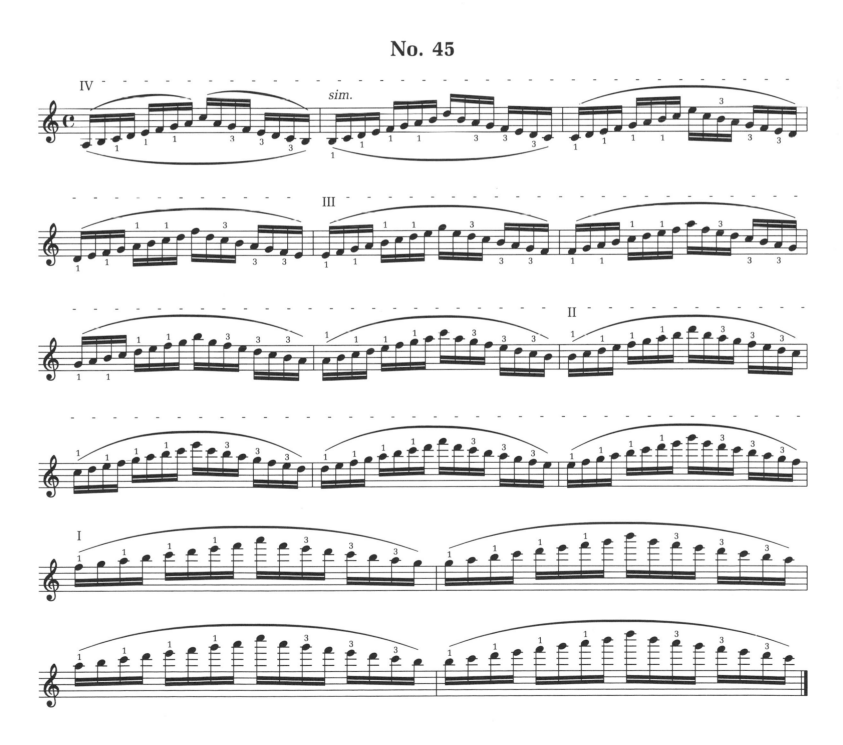

No. 46

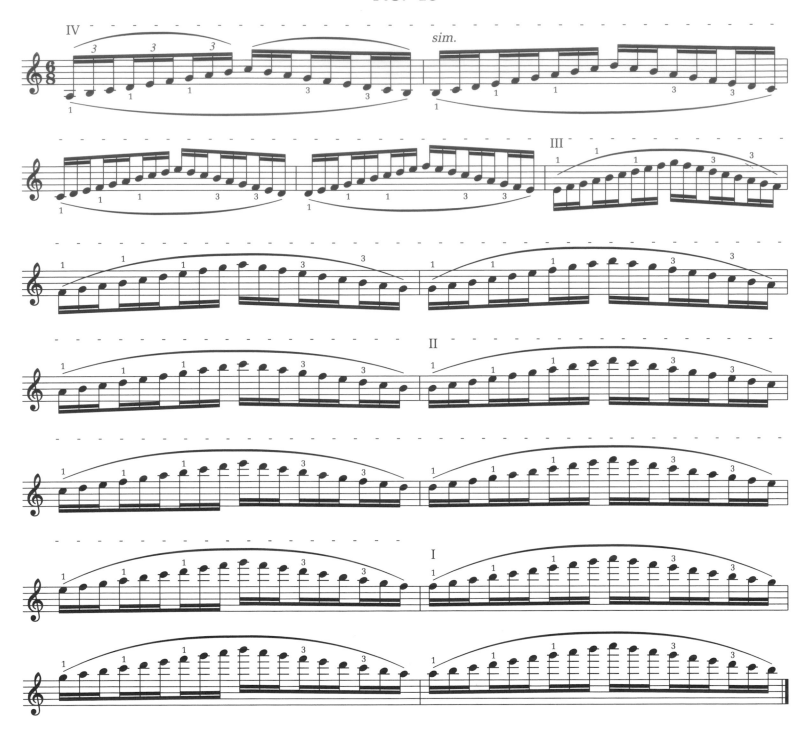

No. 47

Lagenwechsel:	Changes of position:	Changements de position:	Cambiamento di posizione:
von der 1. zur 8., 2. zur 9.,	from 1st to 8th, 2nd to 9th,	de la 1ère à la 8ème, 2ème à 9ème,	dalla 1^a alla 8^a, 2^a alla 9^a,
3. zur 10., u.s.w.	3rd to 10th, etc.	3ème à 10ème, etc.	3^a alla 10^a, ecc.

No. 48

No. 49

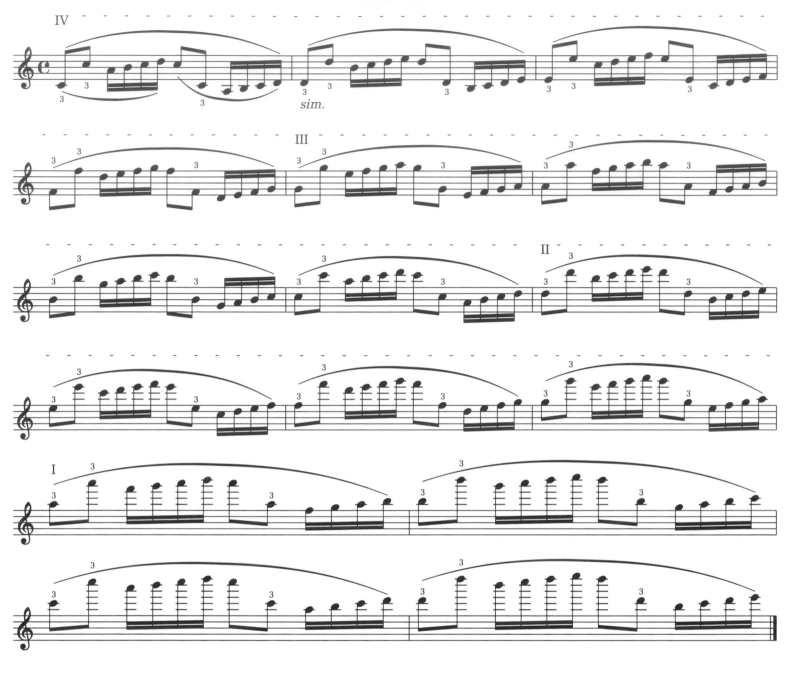

No. 50

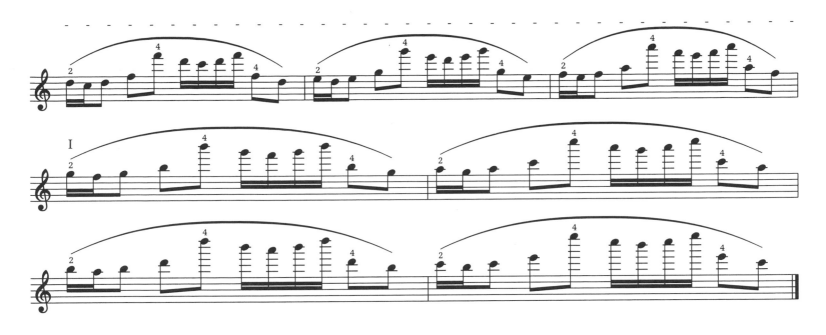

No. 51

No. 52

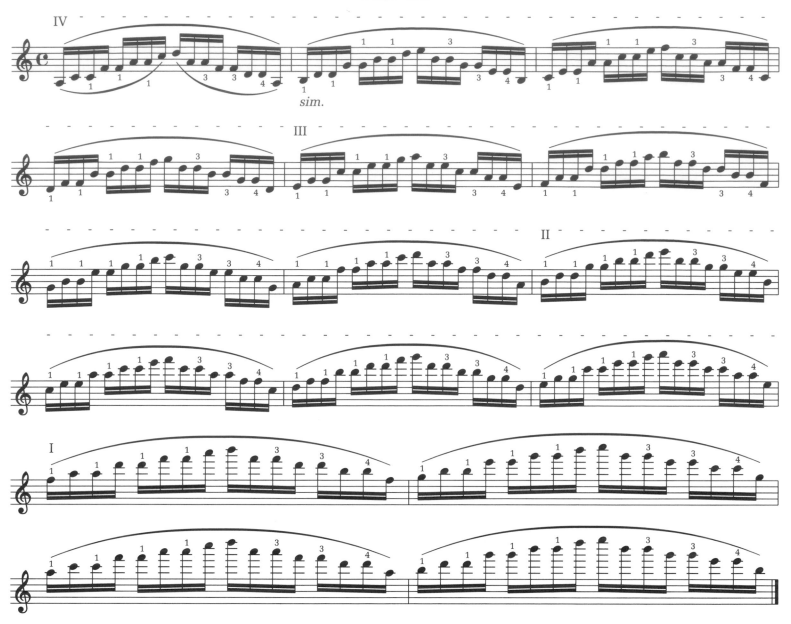

No. 53

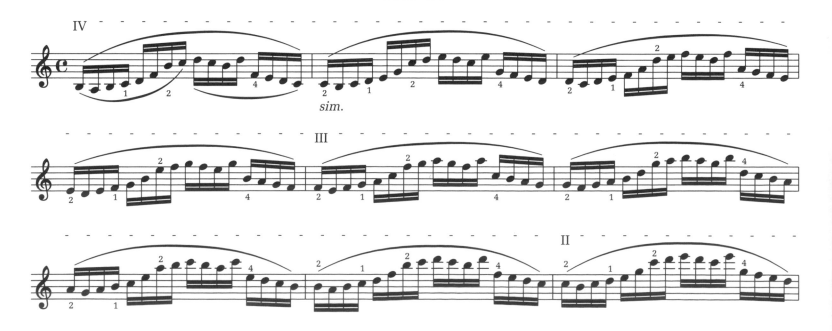

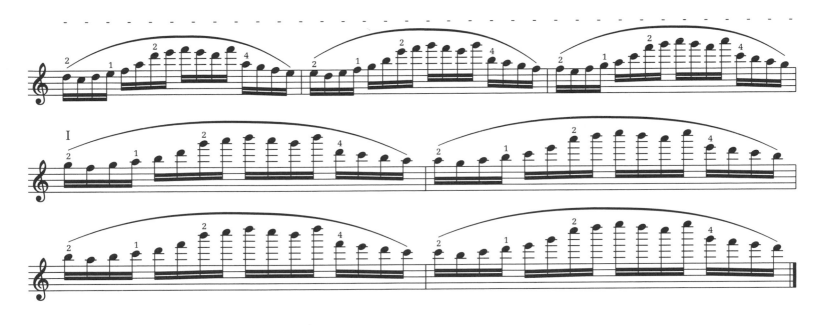

No. 54

No. 55

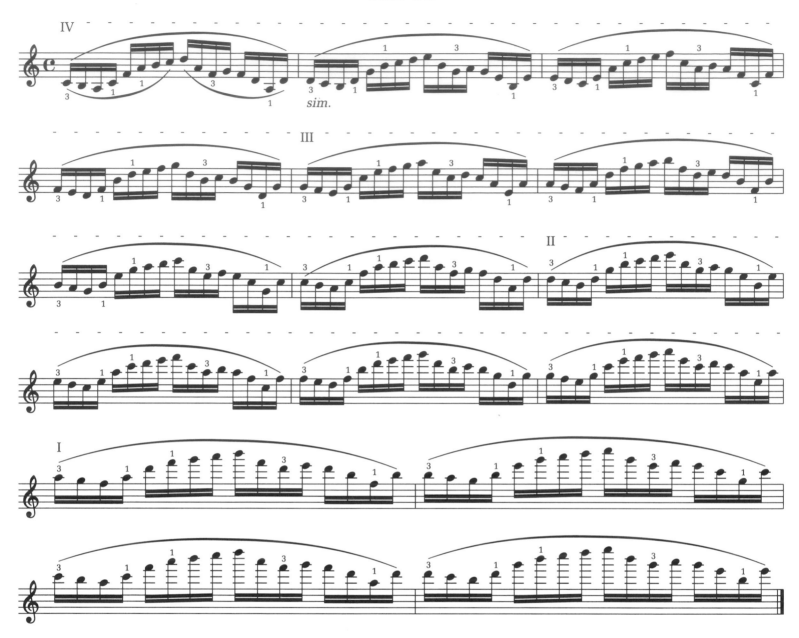

No. 56

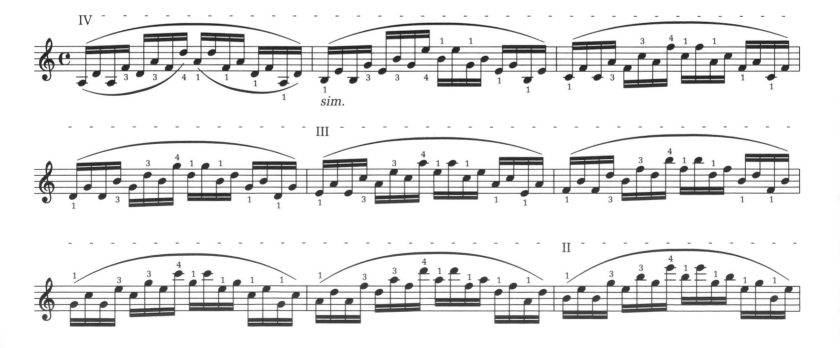

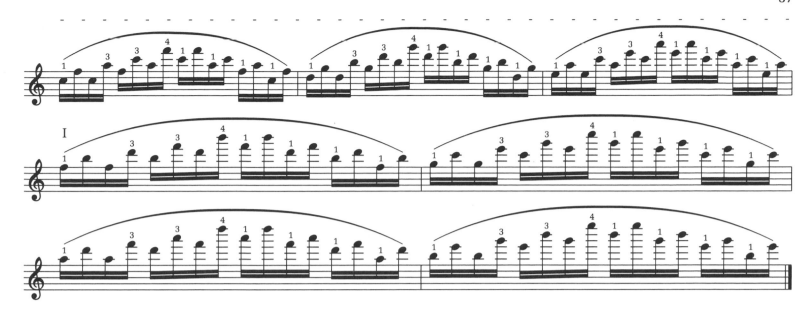

No. 57

| Tonleitern über 3 Oktaven * | Scales across 3 octaves * | Gammes sur 3 octaves * | Scale attraverso 3 ottave * |

C Dur / C major / *do* majeur / Do maggiore

| * Siehe die Anweisungen auf der nächsten Seite. | * See directions on following page. | * Voir directives à la page suivante. | * Vedi istruzioni a pagina seguente. |

38

* Übe Nr. 57–59 in den folgenden Tonarten, legato und staccato:	* Practise Nos. 57–59 in the following keys, legato and staccato:

* Travaillez les Nos. 57 à 59 dans les tonalités suivantes, legato et staccato:	* Studiare dal N. 57 al N. 59 nelle seguenti chiavi, sia legato che staccato:

A moll (harmonisch) / A minor (harmonic) / *la* mineur (harmonique) / La minore (armonica)

G Dur / G major / *sol* majeur / Sol maggiore

E moll / E minor / *mi* mineur / Mi minore

D Dur / D major / *ré* majeur / Re maggiore

H moll / B minor / *si* mineur / Si minore

A Dur / A major / *la* majeur / La maggiore

Fis moll / F# minor / *fa* dièse mineur / Fa diesis minore

E Dur / E major / *mi* majeur / Mi maggiore

Cis moll / C# minor / *do* dièse mineur / Do diesis minore

H Dur / B major / *si* majeur / Si maggiore

Gis moll / G# minor / *sol* dièse mineur / Sol diesis minore

F Dur / F major / *fa* majeur / Fa maggiore

D moll / D minor / *ré* mineur / Re minore

B Dur / B♭ major / *si* bémol majeur / Si bemolle maggiore

G moll / G minor / *sol* mineur / Sol minore

Es Dur / E♭ major / *mi* bémol majeur / Mi bemolle maggiore

C moll / C minor / *do* mineur / Do minore

As Dur / A♭ major / *la* bémol majeur / La bemolle maggiore

F moll / F minor / *fa* mineur / Fa minore

Des Dur / D♭ major / *ré* bémol majeur / Re bemolle maggiore

B moll / B♭ minor / *si* bémol mineur / Si bemolle minore

Ges Dur / G♭ major / *sol* bémol majeur / Sol bemolle maggiore

Es moll / E♭ minor / *mi* bémol mineur / Mi bemolle minore

No. 58

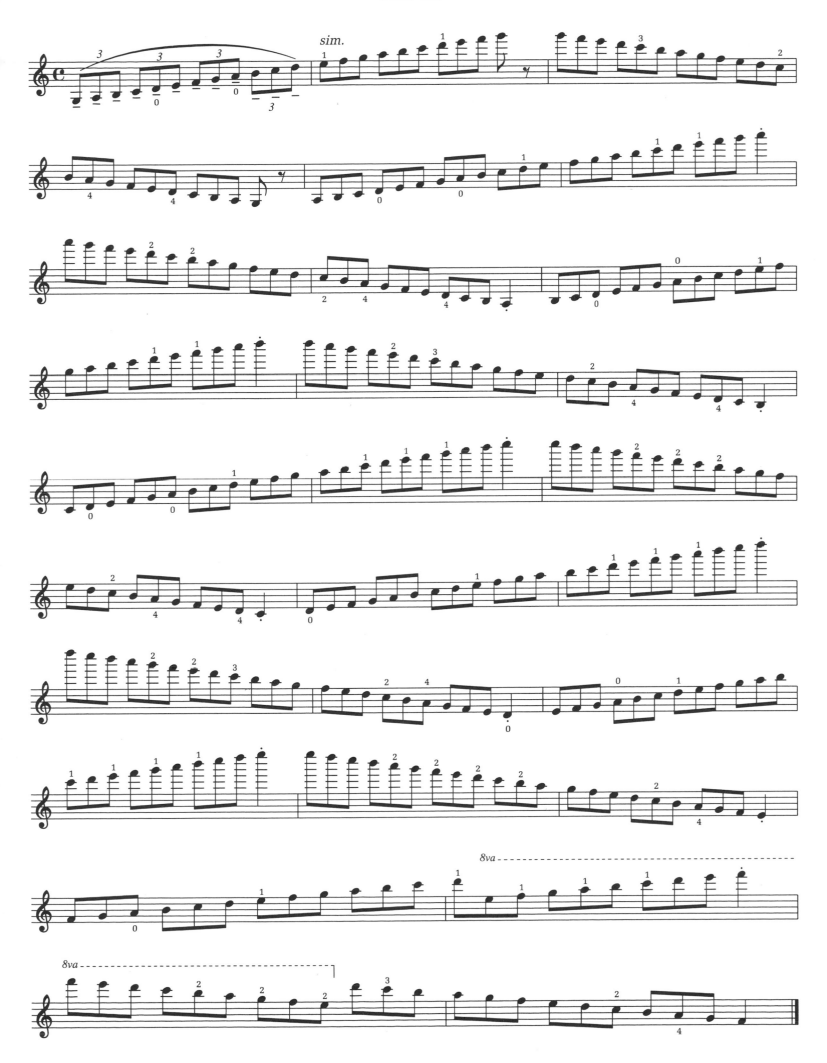

No. 59

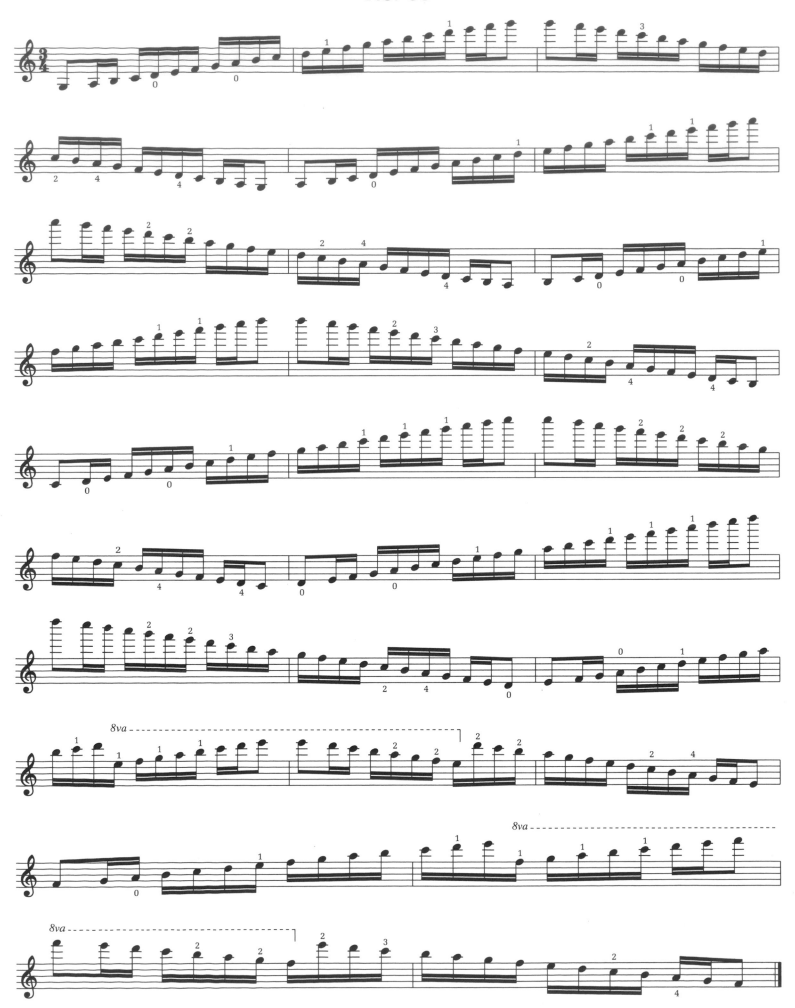